1 2 3 4 5 6 7
3 4 5 6 7 8 9
5 6 7 8 9 10
7 8 9 10 11 12
9 10 12 3 4

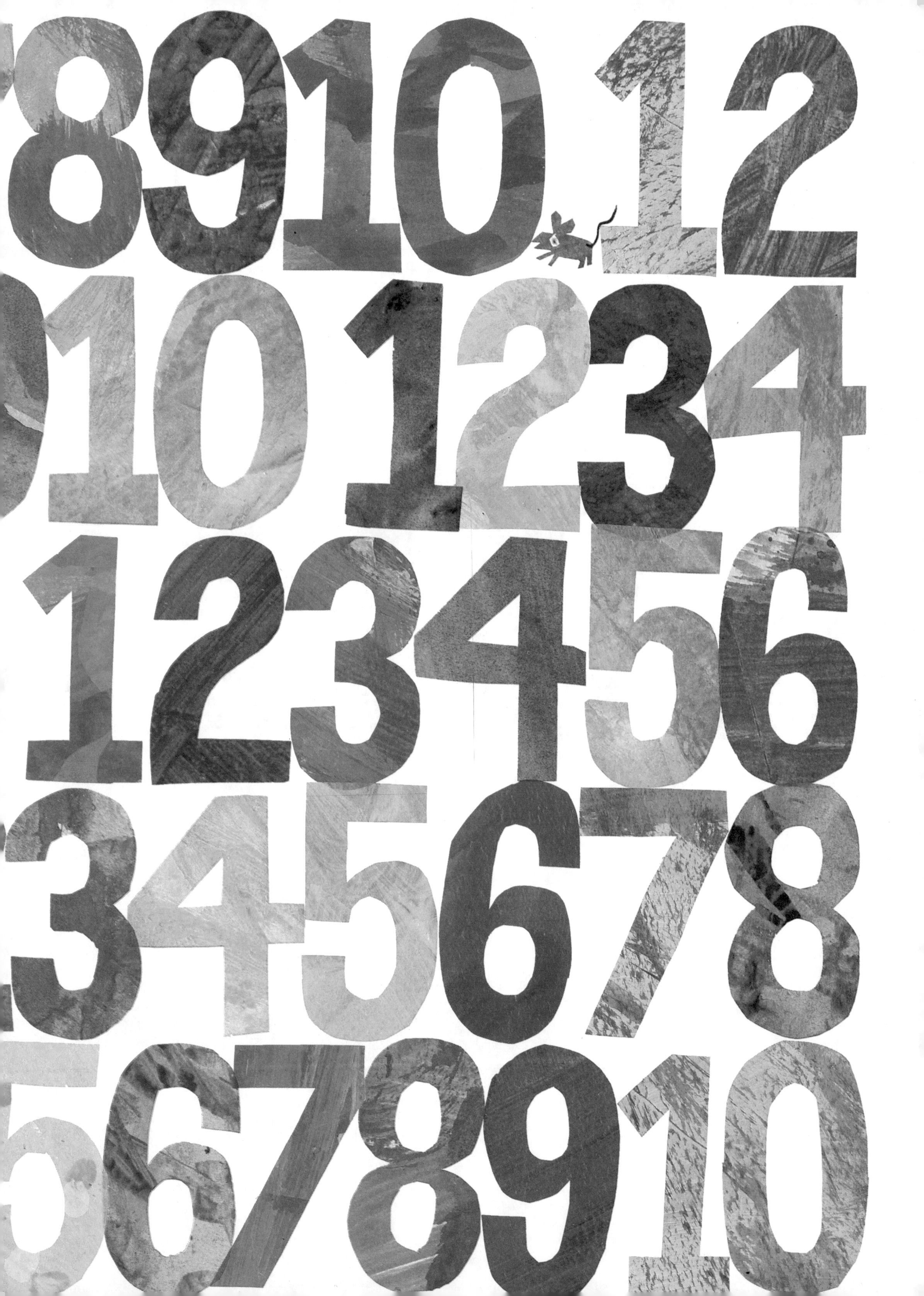
8 9 10 1 2
10 1 2 3 4
1 2 3 4 5 6
3 4 5 6 7 8
6 7 8 9 10

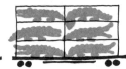

For Cirsten and Rolf

ISBN 0-590-16212-8

12 11 10 9 8 7 6 5   8 9/9 0 1/0

Printed in the U.S.A.

1, 2, 3
TO THE ZOO

a counting book by

ERIC CARLE

1

2

3

10

1234567
345678 9
3456789
5678910
78910 11
910 1234

8910 12
10 1234
123456
345678
678910